A **TRUE** BOOK

D0127842

DO IT YOURSELF **DIY**

Amazing Makerspace

Slippery Slime

CODY CRANE

Children's Press®
An Imprint of Scholastic Inc.

Content Consultant
Jackie Fego
Certified Teacher
C.V. Starr Intermediate School
Brewster, New York

Library of Congress Cataloging-in-Publication Data
Names: Crane, Cody, author.
Title: Amazing makerspace DIY slippery slime / by Cody Crane.
Other titles: Amazing makerspace do-it-yourself slippery slime | Slippery slime | True book.
Description: New York, NY : Children's Press, an imprint of Scholastic, Inc., [2018] |
  Series: A true book | Includes bibliographical references and index.
Identifiers: LCCN 2018002686| ISBN 9780531127353 (library binding) | ISBN 9780531149980 (pbk.)
Subjects: LCSH: Handicraft--Juvenile literature. | Science--Experiments--Juvenile literature. |
  Makerspaces--Juvenile literature.
Classification: LCC TT160 .C83224 2018 | DDC 745.59--dc23
  LC record available at https://lccn.loc.gov/2018002686

All rights reserved. Published in 2019 by Children's Press, an imprint of Scholastic Inc.
Printed in Heshan, China 62

SCHOLASTIC, CHILDREN'S PRESS, A TRUE BOOK™, and associated logos are trademarks and/or registered trademarks of Scholastic Inc., 557 Broadway, New York, NY 10012

2 3 4 5 6 7 8 9 10 R 28 27 26 25 24 23 22 21 20 19

Scholastic Inc., 557 Broadway, New York, NY 10012.

Front cover: Student with Fluffy Slime project

Back cover: Student with Galaxy Slime project

Find the Truth!

Everything you are about to read is true *except* for one of the sentences on this page.

Which one is **TRUE**?

T or F Substances do not change during a chemical reaction.

T or F Slime acts like both a liquid and a solid.

Find the answers in this book.

Contents

Galaxy Slime

Magnetic Slime

Glowing Slime

Fluffy Slime

Safety Note

Some of these
projects use pointy,
sticky, hot, or
otherwise risky objects.
Keep a trusted adult around to
help you out and keep you safe.

You Can Be a Slime Maker!

Makers are always thinking about problems and searching for ways to solve them. They create things and test them out. Then they think about what they have learned and improve their work until it is perfect.

You can be a maker, too! This book will help you make lots of different kinds of slime. Follow the directions to make them in your **makerspace**. Then experiment with your creations to make them even better!

Before You Begin

Follow these safety rules while working on your projects.

1. Work on a clean, flat table or counter. Cover your makerspace with newspaper to keep it clean.

2. Wear old clothes or a smock.

3. Use gloves to protect your hands. Wear goggles when told to do so.

4. When you are done with a project, throw away slime in the trash—NOT the sink. Wash your hands afterward.

And remember: Always ask for an adult's permission before using household products.

Galaxy Slime

Slime is a strange substance. It is not quite a liquid and not quite a solid. However, like all things, this squishy and stretchy stuff is made up of **matter**. In this project you'll make slime that glitters like the Milky Way—the galaxy where our solar system is found. The Milky Way contains billions of swirling, twinkling stars.

Every star we see in the night sky is part of the Milky Way galaxy.

What Is Matter?

Matter makes up everything around us. The tiniest pieces of matter are called **atoms**. Most matter comes in one of three types: solid, liquid, or gas. A solid has tightly packed atoms, so it keeps its shape. Because a liquid's atoms easily slide past one another, it can take the shape of the container it is in. Gases contain atoms that move freely. They will spread out to fill a given space.

This illustration shows how atoms are arranged differently in different types of matter.

solid

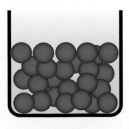

liquid

gas

Slime sometimes acts like a liquid, but it's very different from other liquids, like water.

A Liquid or a Solid?

Slime changes the way it behaves under different conditions. When you roll slime into a ball, it holds its shape like a solid. When you stop rolling the slime, it oozes through your fingers like a liquid. Scientists call substances like slime **non-Newtonian fluids**. Any force, like a squeeze, causes the slime's particles to tangle up. As a result, the slime stiffens and becomes more solid. When no force is applied, the particles flow like a liquid.

Make Galaxy Slime

TOOLS

Three small mixing bowls

Plastic spoon or flat wooden craft stick

Paper plate

Measuring spoons

Measuring cup

MATERIALS

1/4 cup cornstarch

Cornstarch acts as a base for the slime.

1 tablespoon glitter

The small, shiny plastic pieces in glitter reflect light to make the slime shimmer.

4 teaspoons shampoo

This thick liquid binds to particles of cornstarch. That holds the slime together.

Food coloring

Food coloring is a dye that colors the slime. You'll need three colors, such as blue, green, and pink.

Project Instructions

1. Pour the cornstarch into one of the bowls.

2. Sprinkle the glitter on top of the cornstarch in the bowl.

3. Add the shampoo to the bowl. Slowly stir everything together. If the mixture is too dry, add more shampoo. If it's too wet, add more cornstarch.

5. Divide the slime evenly among the three bowls. Mix in a few drops of food coloring—a different color for each bowl.

4. Stir until combined. Then knead the slime with your hands to mix completely.

Slime can be stored in an airtight container.

Squish and Test It!

Roll each colored slime into a tube. Lay the tubes side by side on a paper plate and then twist them together. Roll the slime into a ball. It should hold its shape like a solid. Let it drip from your hand. It should flow like a liquid.

Change It!

Experiment with some of the following changes. What new results do you see?

- Add more glitter to your slime.
- Make slime with more colors, and add them in.
- Add other objects to your slime, like beads, sequins, confetti stars, or tiny foam balls.

Results: The glittier slime is less slippery; the colors blend together more; some objects mix into the slime better than others.

Fluffy Slime

Slime recipes start with simple ingredients that can be powdery, sticky, or soapy. But when you mix them together, how they look and feel changes. The ingredients transform into a brand-new substance you can stretch, squish, and squeeze. What causes these everyday ingredients to turn into slime?

A **chemical reaction**. You can see how this works for yourself in this project. You will change common household supplies into super-fluffy slime.

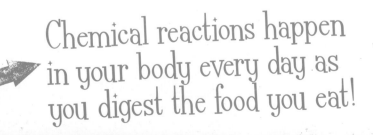

Chemical reactions happen in your body every day as you digest the food you eat!

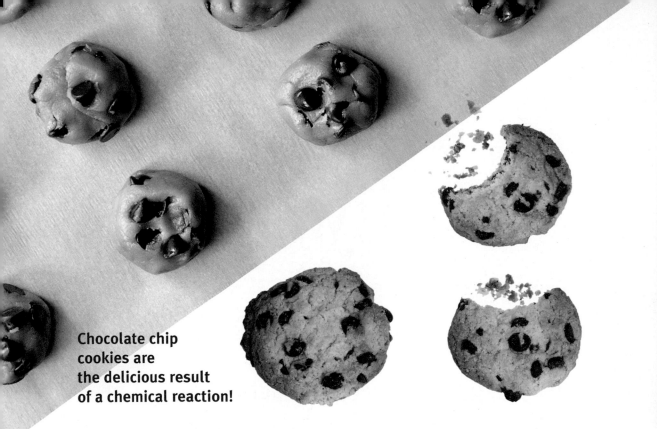

Chocolate chip cookies are the delicious result of a chemical reaction!

Chemical Reactions

Most substances are made up of atoms linked together to form **molecules**. During a chemical reaction, these molecules change to create brand-new substances. Baking is an example of a chemical reaction. You combine your ingredients and bake them. What comes out of the oven is something completely different from what went in!

Polymers

One way to make slime is with glue. This sticky substance is made up of long molecules called **polymers**. Glue's polymers are big. But they can still slip and slide past each other. That is why glue is thick but runny. A chemical reaction takes place when you add certain chemicals to glue. Bonds form between glue's polymers, connecting them. They now have a much harder time moving around. As a result, the glue becomes goopy. It is now slime!

A polymer is a long molecule that is mostly made up of many repeating units.

19

Make Fluffy Slime

TOOLS

Medium mixing bowl

Plastic spoon or flat wooden craft stick

Measuring cup

Measuring spoons

MATERIALS

4 ounces school glue

Glue acts as the base for the slime.

3 tablespoons contact lens solution

Contact lens solution contains borax, which triggers a chemical reaction in the glue.

1 cup shaving cream

Shaving cream is foamy. Foam gives the slime a fluffy texture.

Food coloring

Food coloring is a dye that colors the slime.

Project Instructions

1. Pour the glue into the bowl.

2. Use the spoon or craft stick to scoop the shaving cream into the bowl.

3. Add a few drops of food coloring and the contact lens solution to the bowl.

5. Use your hands to knead and stretch the slime until it's no longer sticky. Be patient; this may take several minutes.

4. Stir the ingredients together. Keep mixing until everything is combined.

Squish and Test It!

Squeeze your fluffy slime. It should feel light and wobbly. If not, keep stretching and kneading until the slime feels smooth. Poke your fingers into your slime. You should hear tiny popping sounds—that's the bubbles in the foam bursting.

Change It!

Experiment with some of the following changes. What new results do you see?

- Mix in another cup of shaving cream.
- Let the slime sit covered overnight.
- Cover the slime and freeze it for 15 minutes.

Results: It will become foamier; bubbles will have risen and popped, so the top will have a dimpled texture and the slime will be less foamy; the slime won't stretch or wobble as easily.

Slimy Creatures

Many living things—including people—make slime. Creatures use the gooey stuff to protect themselves, get around, and snag food.

achEWW!

The inside of your nose is coated in **mucus**, also known as snot. This sticky substance traps germs and other tiny particles when you breathe in. That stops them from reaching your lungs and keeps you from getting sick.

Slippery Fish

Hagfish are eel-like animals that live in the ocean. They can make four cups of slime in a fraction of a second! If a hagfish is attacked, a lot of slime oozes from its skin. This makes the fish hard to grab, allowing it to escape.

Snail Trail

The bellies of snails and slugs are coated in slime, which allows the animals to glide more easily over surfaces. The slime is not just slippery. It is also sticky. That allows snails and slugs to climb vertically up surfaces without falling off.

Sticky Spit

A chameleon catches bugs using its superlong tongue, which can stretch twice the length of the animal's body. The end of a chameleon's tongue is covered in slimy spit that sticks to insects. The chameleon just has to slurp its tongue back into its mouth to reel in a tasty meal.

Cave Snot

Some cave walls drip with slime. It is made by millions of tiny microbes, creatures too small to see with the naked eye. The slime protects the microbes and gives them a place to live.

CHAPTER 3

Magnetic Slime

Many types of slime wiggle when you give them a shake. In this project, you will create slime that seems to move on its own—no jiggling or poking required. You will even see the slime stretch out gooey arms to grab objects. But don't worry—the slime is not alive. And there is nothing magical going on. So how does it work? The secret behind this slime is the power of **magnetism**.

 Like a magnet, the Earth has its own magnetic field.

Magnets

A magnet is an object surrounded by a magnetic field. This field is invisible, but it produces a force that can be felt by other objects. The force attracts anything that contains certain metals, like iron. These objects get pulled toward the magnet, and the magnet gets pulled toward them. Magnets are not attracted to materials like glass, plastic, or wood.

Can you guess why this is called a horseshoe magnet?

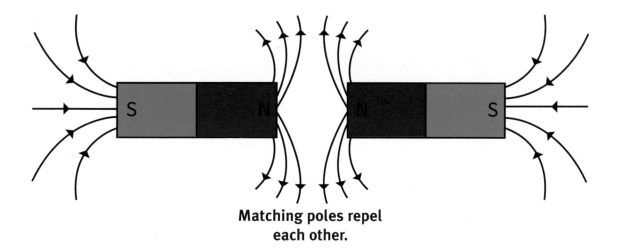

**Matching poles repel
each other.**

North and South

Magnets themselves contain metals like iron, so they can also affect other magnets. All magnets have two **poles**, or ends. The poles, called north and south, are where a magnet creates the strongest force. If you touch the poles of two magnets together, one of two things can happen: Opposite poles, one north and one south, will attract. Matching poles, both north or both south, will repel, or push away, each other.

29

Make Magnetic Slime

TOOLS

Paper plate

Plastic spoon or flat wooden craft stick

Measuring cup

Measuring spoons

MATERIALS

1/4 cup school glue

Glue acts as the base for the slime.

2 teaspoons laundry detergent

Detergent contains borax, which triggers a chemical reaction in the glue.

1 tablespoon iron filings

Iron filings are made up of small flakes of iron. Magnets are attracted to this metal.

regular

neodymium

Magnets

Magnets are surrounded by an invisible force field that attracts the iron filings.

Project Instructions

1. Put on your safety goggles.

2. Pour the glue onto the plate.

3. Sprinkle the iron filings into the glue. Stir until all the filings are mixed into the glue.

31

5. Use your hands to knead and stretch the slime until it has a smooth texture. Next, you will test it with a magnet.

4. Stir in the detergent.

Squish and Test It!

Hold a magnet just above the slime on the plate. It should grab onto the magnet! If not, try again using a neodymium magnet, which can be found at a hardware store. It has a much stronger pull than a regular magnet does.

Change It!

Experiment with some of the following changes. What new results do you see?

- Add another tablespoon of iron filings.
- Stick multiple magnets together—regular and neodymium—and put them near your slime.

Results: The magnet will grab even more slime; the magnets will be stronger—they'll be more attracted to the slime, and the slime to them. Neodymium creates the strongest pulling force of types of magnets.

Glowing Slime

You just read about some real-life examples of slime. That includes the mucus inside your own nose! In this project, you can make slime that looks and feels a lot like actual snot. This maker creation may seem gross—that's what makes it fun. But this slime does something real boogers do not. Thanks to a special ingredient, it glows in the dark.

 Sunlight can recharge glow-in-the-dark objects that are out of energy.

Glow Power

Many products can glow in the dark, including toys, stickers, clothing, and paint. They all work using a process called **phosphorescence**. Chemicals in the objects soak up light from their surroundings. Then they slowly give off that energy as a glow.

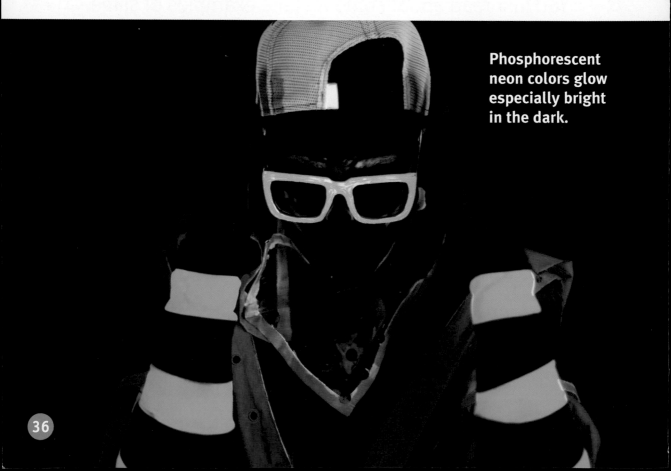

Phosphorescent neon colors glow especially bright in the dark.

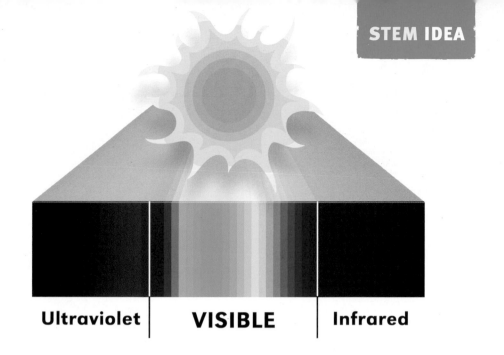

| Ultraviolet | VISIBLE | Infrared |

Invisible Light

The sun gives off light we can see, called visible light. It may look white, but it actually contains all the colors of the rainbow. The sun also gives off light we cannot see. One type is infrared light. The other is called **ultraviolet light**—high-energy rays that charge up glow-in-the-dark objects, including your slime. Some lightbulbs also give off ultraviolet light. But it is a very small amount compared to that given off by the sun.

Make Glowing Slime

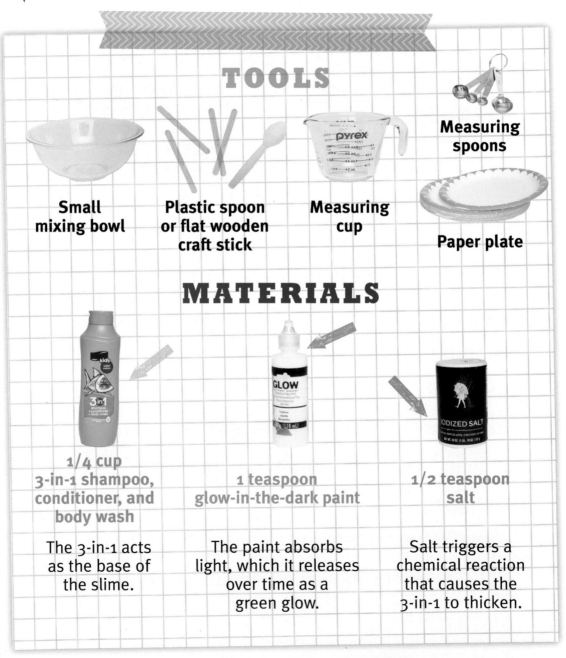

TOOLS

Small mixing bowl

Plastic spoon or flat wooden craft stick

Measuring cup

Measuring spoons

Paper plate

MATERIALS

1/4 cup 3-in-1 shampoo, conditioner, and body wash

The 3-in-1 acts as the base of the slime.

1 teaspoon glow-in-the-dark paint

The paint absorbs light, which it releases over time as a green glow.

1/2 teaspoon salt

Salt triggers a chemical reaction that causes the 3-in-1 to thicken.

Project Instructions

1. Pour the 3-in-1 into the bowl.

2. Mix in the paint.

3. Sprinkle the salt over the mixture in the bowl.

4. Stir until the mixture begins to look and feel like jelly.

5. Transfer the mixture to a paper plate and let it sit in direct sunlight for one minute.

Squish and Test It!

Place your slime in a dark room. Watch it glow! The paint you used is phosphorescent. It released energy from the sun as a bright glow. If you don't see a glow, place your slime in the sunlight for a longer time. Then try it again.

Change It!

Experiment with some of the following changes. What new results do you see?

- Leave your slime in a dark place overnight.
- Use indoor LED, fluorescent, and incandescent bulbs to charge your slime.

Results: Your slime will no longer glow; LEDs and incandescent bulbs don't give off enough UV light to charge glow-in-the-dark objects, but fluorescent bulbs do.

Slimeline

The toy now called Silly Putty is invented by accident by a scientist who is trying to create a substitute for rubber.

The toy company Mattel starts selling green Slime for kids.

1943 ▶ **1949** ▶ **1976** ▶ **1979** ▶

Dr. Seuss writes *Bartholomew and the Oobleck*, about a boy who saves the world from a slime called oobleck.

The kids' cable channel Nickelodeon becomes famous for dumping slime on kids and adults alike on TV.

In the cartoon series *Teenage Mutant Ninja Turtles*, toxic slime turns ordinary turtles into superheroes.

Videos showing makers creating homemade slime become a hit online.

1984　▶　**1987**　▶　**1992**　▶　**2016**　▶

Mattel releases a goopy toy called Gak based on Nickelodeon's popular slime.

A slime-covered ghost named Slimer is featured in the movie *Ghostbusters*.

True Statistics

Amount of snot on average a person produces a day: 1.5 quarts (1.4 liters)

Weight of the largest slime ever made: 13,820 pounds (6,269 kilograms)

Number of subscribers to popular slime maker Karina Garcia's YouTube channel: more than 7 million

Amount of Silly Putty sold each year: more than 90 tons

Amount of slime used during Nickelodeon's Kids' Choice Awards since the show began in 1987: more than 230,000 gallons (870,645 liters)

Did you find the truth?

(T) Slime acts like both a liquid and a solid.

(F) Substances do not change during a chemical reaction.

Resources

Books

Basher, Simon. Chemistry: *Getting a Big Reaction*. London: Kingfisher, 2010.

DK. *The Slime Book*. New York: DK Publishing, 2017.

Twist, Clint. A *Little Book of Slime*. Ontario: Firefly Books, 2012.

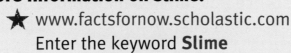

Visit this Scholastic Web site for more information on slime:
www.factsfornow.scholastic.com
Enter the keyword **Slime**

Important Words

atoms (AT-uhmz) the smallest units of matter

chemical reaction (KEM-i-kuhl ree-AK-shuhn) when substances undergo a change to form new substances

magnetism (MAG-ni-tiz-uhm) the attractive property of magnets

makerspace (MAY-kur-spays) any place where people plan, design, tinker, create, change, and fix things for fun or to solve problems

matter (MAT-er) any substance that has mass and takes up space

molecules (MOL-uh-kyoolz) two or more atoms bonded together

mucus (MYOO-kuhs) a slimy substance made by living things

non-Newtonian fluids (NON-noo-TOH-nee-uhn FLOO-ids) fluids whose ability to flow changes depending on the forces applied to them

phosphorescence (fos-fuh-RES-uhnts) the ability to absorb and slowly release light energy

poles (pohlz) each end of a magnet

polymers (pol-UH-merz) large molecules made up of repeating units

ultraviolet light (uhl-truh-VAHY-uh-lit lahyt) invisible, high-energy light rays

Index

Page numbers in **bold** indicate illustrations.

About the Author

Cody Crane is an award-winning writer of nonfiction for children. From a young age, she was set on becoming a scientist. She later discovered that writing about science could be just as fun as the real thing. She lives in Houston, Texas, with her husband and son.

Thanks!

Scholastic Library Publishing wants to especially thank all the children who worked as models in this book for their time and generosity.

PHOTOGRAPHS ©: 5 graph paper and throughout: billnoll/iStockphoto; 11: jarabee123/Getty Images; 12 wooden sticks and throughout: I am Kulz/Shutterstock; 18 left cookies: marla dawn studio/Shutterstock; 18 right cookies: ppart/Shutterstock; 19: Vicki Beaver/Alamy Images; 24 left: junko/Getty Images; 24 right: R Koenig/age fotostock; 24-25 slime: Anastasiia_M/iStockphoto; 25 top left: Tony Hamblin/FLPA/Minden Pictures; 25 top right: Laurent Geslin/NPL/Minden Pictures; 25 center: Kurit afshen/Shutterstock; 25 bottom: Robbie Shone/Getty Images; 28: Claire Cordier/Getty Images; 29: photoiconix/Shutterstock; 30 bottom left iron filings: xpixel/Shutterstock; 30 bottom right round magnet: photoiconix/Shutterstock; 30 bottom right iron filings: Martin Leigh/Getty Images; 36: studioda/iStockphoto; 37 EM spectrum: Fouad A. Saad/Shutterstock; 37 sun: Panda Vector/Shutterstock; 40 grass: Ewa Studio/Shutterstock; 42 top right: Paul Orr/Shutterstock; 42 bottom left: Random House/http://www.seussville.com/Wikipedia; 42 bottom right: Christopher Polk/KCA2012/Getty Images; 43 top left phone: Denis Rozhnovsky/Shutterstock; 43 top right screen: Nathan Congleton/NBC/NBCU Photo Bank/Getty Images; 43 center left: AF archive/Alamy Images; 43 bottom left: AF archive/Alamy Images; 43 bottom right: jarabee123/Getty Images; 44: jarabee123/Getty Images.

All other images © Bianca Alexis Photography.